Introduction

Stone, n. piece of rock of any shape and of no great size. rock, n. solid part of earth's crust, large detached stone or boulder.

These prosaic dictionary definitions seem an inadequate description of the wondrous array of rocks and minerals all around us.

Walking along a pebble beach or beside a stony brook searching for just that special stone can be an absorbing occupation. It is fascinating to ponder on the geological journey that brought it to a particular location. Always an enjoyable pastime, wonderfully relaxing and at times an unusual or special find can be most exhilarating. Many people have their particular favourites from shiny black stones to pure white opaque ones, polished smooth by the constant pounding of the sea. Heart shaped stones, pebbles with holes, some that contain silver quartz sparkle alongside others that display a myriad of colours may be the fascination.

Collecting stones and rocks can represent a variety of memories of countries and special places visited, whereas others can provide inspiration for a number of decorative projects. Textural surfaces, intricate patterns, markings, dimensional layering and subtle colour schemes can inform and inspire many design starting points for the designer and creative stitcher. Understanding how rocks and stones were made over millions of years can increase your awareness and focus. Rocks were forged in the explosive energy of the earth's creation. They have solidified from molten chemical cauldrons into some of the most diverse, dramatic and beautiful structures in the world. Over millions of years they have

continued to evolve through constant upheavals, crushing and impacting, fracturing and squeezing by the evolutionary earth movements.
The Grand Canyon is breathtaking in it's sheer size and spectacle. It is awe inspiring to realise that these formations have been caused mainly by the force of water.
Combined with the sun, the extreme temperatures cause fissures, faults, holes and cracks in an infinite variety of patterns and qualities of surface.
Fossil forms sandwiched between layers of rock tell the story of ancient times.

We can use these elements in our work with textiles. Sections observed and then recorded out of context is always a good way to start. By looking carefully at the surfaces using a pencil, pen or stick and ink (Book 12) draw what you see. A number of unexpected elements may well come to the fore. The corrosive action of nature in rocks and minerals has a structured logic. By drawing and observation this can enhance our aesthetic awareness and sense of colour, texture and proportion.

Describing the surfaces will also help to suggest appropriate techniques to use.
Organic, eroded, ridged, crevassed, fissured, craggy, indented, striated, holey, sparkly, rough and shiny are all words that immediately bring particular surfaces to mind. Any of these elements can be exaggerated or understated to develop the intended design and increase individuality.
Fabrics and materials that respond to heat can be developed to describe rock like distortions. Fissures may be created by etching into fabric in a number of ways.

Precious stones are prized for their colour and quality but semi-precious stones often have more scope for drawing and design. The personal aspect of a birthstone could be a good place to start.Myths and legends based on stones may also prove fascinating.

With the whole world at our feet, it may still be wise to start looking nearer to home and find the possibilities in some humble pebbles that on close inspection contain wonderfully subtle colours and patterns.

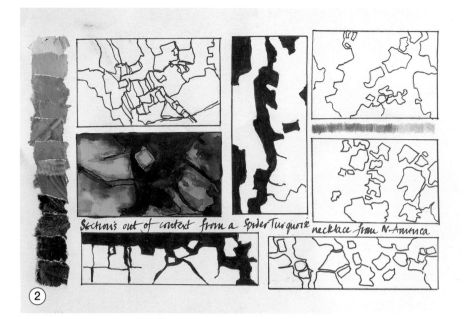

Sections out of context from a Spider Turquoise necklace from N-America

① ②

create a textile necklace based on the patterns and colours in the original. (see page 22)

Gemstones may also have a birthday significance that could be a good source of personal imagery for you or your family. Turquoise happens to be the Christmas stone and is derived from 'The Turkish Stone' or 'Luck Stone'. The Aztecs described it as a stone of the Gods and thought that turquoise amulets tied to weapons would improve their effectiveness. A study of stones and their various symbolic or mythical associations could prove fruitful.

Close to Home - Gemstones

Jewellery collections almost invariably contain stones either precious or semi-precious. Agates, amethysts, turquoise, lapis lazulae and many others are rich sources of inspiration (Caption 1 above right). A magnifying glass will help to see the patterns and structures with more clarity. Greatly enlarged photocopies or scanned computer images will also help to reveal the fabulous patterns.

The opposite page features a necklace and bracelet of spider turquoise containing patterns and colours that may be exploited in many different textile techniques. To start it may be helpful to cut a range of paper windows to place over the stones and see the patterns out of context. It is a well tried and tested method but effective and so worth remembering.

By looking at different shapes and formats, wide and narrow, square and rectangular etc, possibilities begin to emerge. It is often best to start with thumbnail sketches and record just the main lines, making colour notes with torn magazine papers or colour pencils (see fig 2 above).

The square cushions illustrated below were designed using this method. The synthetic velvet was coloured with transfer paints and bonded to the background before being stitched down and further enriched with surface stitch. The soft beads have been dry felted using wool tops to

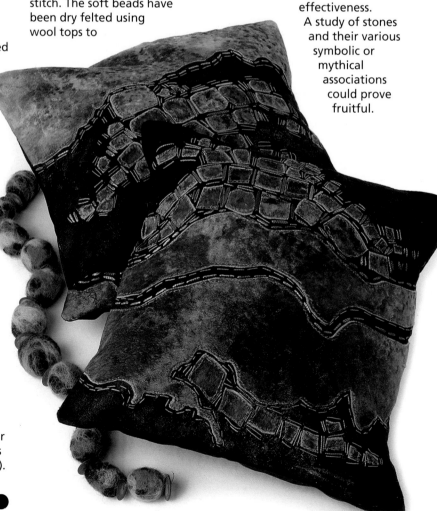

Stone Resist Dyeing

Stones may be a bane to gardeners but even the most unpromising selection can be used to good effect.
Whilst they may display lovely patterns and textures they can be used to distort cloth.

Over centuries people have used stones to pound cloth for softening and cleaning. Even now, stones can be used to distress and age fabrics for theatrical and fashion effects. The fabrics displayed here have been patterned by using stones tied into the fabric to act as a resist to the dyeing process.

Irregular pebbles create unusual shapes and can be used to good effect. Avoid very sharp stones as they may damage the fabric. Traditionally, shapes were tied with string or twine but rubber bands can be most effective and easier to handle. (fig 1 above) The techniques are fairly straight forward but there are some basic guidelines to help.

• The dyes used here are hot water dyes available in most local stores.

• Always handle dyes with care and it is advisable to wear protective gloves.

• Work from lighter colours through to darker, when using more than one colour.

• Wash the fabric first to get rid of the dressing.

• Decide on the base colour. If you do not want white or other base colour of your fabric then dye the whole fabric first.

• Most of the fabrics here were pre-dyed to avoid white areas.

• Decide where you want the patterning and work methodically by binding the stones tightly into the cloth with rubber bands or string.

• Wet the tied fabric and place in the dye bath following the manufacturer's instructions carefully, particularly the addition of salt to ensure colour fastness.

• When dyed, rinse thoroughly until the water runs clear.

• At this point you could untie the stones and you would have two colours, the base colour and the second colour with the resist stone patterns.

• More complex colours and patterns can be achieved by adding further stones or increasing the width of the existing tied areas. (fig 2 right)

• Two packets of black have been used as the third colour to ensure a good saturated final effect.

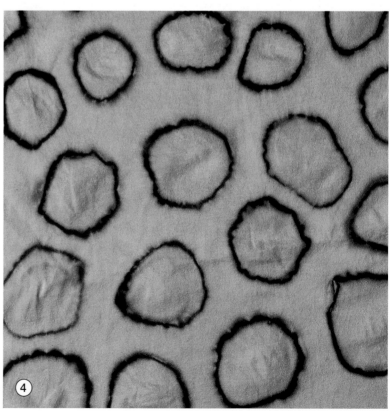

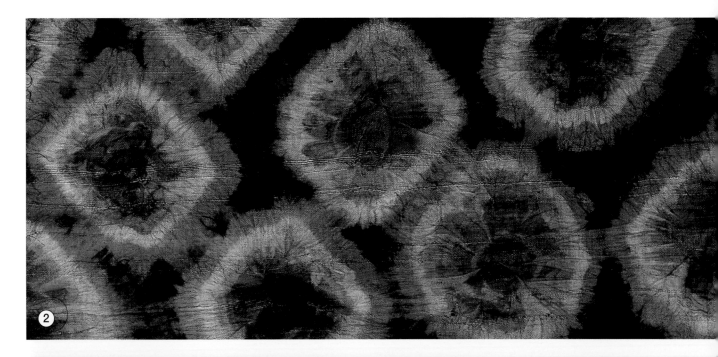

②

• When dyed and thoroughly rinsed after the last colour, carefully unwrap the bands or string. If using scissors be very careful not to cut the fabric as this is easily done.

• When dry, the fabric may be ironed.

These cloths make wonderful scarves, accessories, cushions etc. Used for patchwork and quilting they could become a colourful addition to the palette. Surface stitching needs careful consideration to enrich and not overwhelm. A richly dimensional

effect will happen when the cloth is left to dry thoroughly before untying. Fig 3 (top left) shows a piece of resist dyed silk with the stone shapes firmly moulded into the fabric. Because it is silk it needs careful handling and delicate washing to retain this undulating surface. More permanent patterning can be achieved when using polyester fabric. (see page 6)

An interesting alternative to the stone resist cloths could be achieved by discharging the colour rather than adding it.

Fig 4 (left) has been worked on black T-shirt cotton with bound stones to form the pattern. The whole piece was dipped into bleach to discharge the black. Great care must be taken to wear a mask and use gloves. Depending on the composition of the black, subtle colours are revealed and the cloth can be removed as soon as the desired effect has been achieved. The fabric has been immersed in vinegar to neutralise the bleach before washing. After a final rinsing in water the stones were released and a negative pattern revealed.

Dimensional Resist & Transfer Painting

There has been considerable interest recently in dimensional resist dyeing. It takes many forms and the traditional Japanese Shibori technique has been much vaunted.
Unlike cotton and silk, polyester has the facility of changing its shape more permanently. The dying can be more difficult with this fibre and it may be a good idea to colour it before resist dying.

Transfer paints work really well on Polyester and as we have mentioned in previous books they can be so exciting and versatile that we wonder why they are still little used. (see Book 4)
This is an opportunity to use some very dramatic effects to achieve organic rock like structures. Textures sponged and stippled onto thin paper to form textural drifts of colour can be a good starting point.

Splattering paint (1) and blowing it through a straw (2) are just two of the techniques used here to represent rock surfaces.
The application of transfer paints to wet or crumpled paper will result in organic patterns and rocky effects.
Similarly, crumple the fabric before ironing and dramatic shapes will be revealed.

The rock formations in the two illustrations (shown top right) are achieved by applying generous amounts of transfer paint to paper and whilst still wet laying a layer of crumpled cling wrap onto the surface. As the paint slowly dries it pools into the fissures and cracks so imitative of stone structures. On the left is the transfer paper and right the polyester print from it.
Layers of different papers working from light to dark offer the possibility of complex imagery that can inspire a range of stitched cloths.

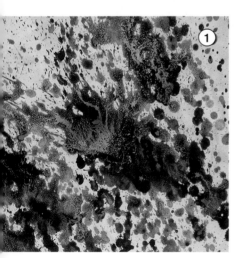

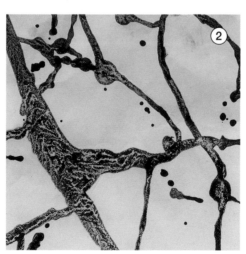

Right:
Transfer painted polyester fabric was first tied with stones before being steamed in a pressure cooker for 20 minutes before drying and untying.

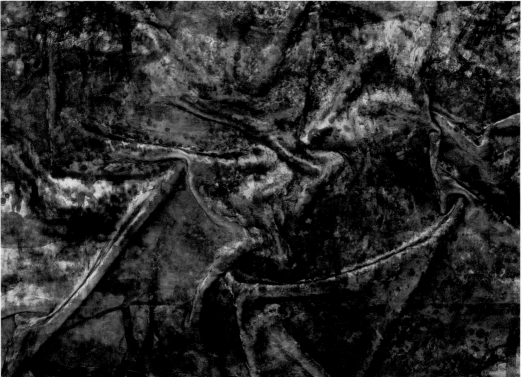

Above:
Several layers of splattering and textured papers were over printed to achieve this richly patterned synthetic velvet.

Silk Painting

Stones can inspire amazing designs and subtle colour schemes and when they are wet they display a vibrant intensified colour range.

By observing carefully and describing the main shapes, lines and colours, these aspects can be adapted by repeating, elongating or contriving to fit required shapes. Some of the sketches shown illustrate the primary shapes taken out of context and placed lengthways into casual but not exact repeating units and lines.

As already stated, the close observation of rocks and stones will reveal unusual colour combinations, subtle nuances and textured marks. These can provide design 'stepping stones' and colour fabrics for such items as

cushions, scarves or material for appliqué, quilting or patchwork items. Every one needs to refresh their store or palette of colour schemes from time to time other wise predictable colourways may prevail.

Ready made scarves and an extensive range of iron fix silk paints are easily purchased from specialist shops advertising in embroidery or textile magazines. Books and magazine articles continue to describe and encourage readers to try out various techniques using outliners, salt effects, wax resist and so on.

Silk paint is designed to be used on silk fabrics but it can be used to colour other materials and iron fixed as usual. Dampening the cloth will help to spread the

colour rather than leave a hard-edged 'tide' mark depending on the desired effect.

The silk scarves illustrated show marks and blemishes reflecting some characteristics observed on stones. Set designs with outlined colours did not seem appropriate although stylised, hard edged patterns could be created from the information collected. Many of the scarves were overprinted with a diluted grey or purple wash of silk paint to tone down or blend in the colours for a more subtle effect. On some, clear water was applied to dilute the colour in organic splodges and lines.

A 'low tech' approach was deliberately chosen. The scarves were not stretched over a frame but laid flat over wall lining paper and news print. Having mixed the colour and made decisions about the main imagery to be created, the paint was applied with sponges and brushes.

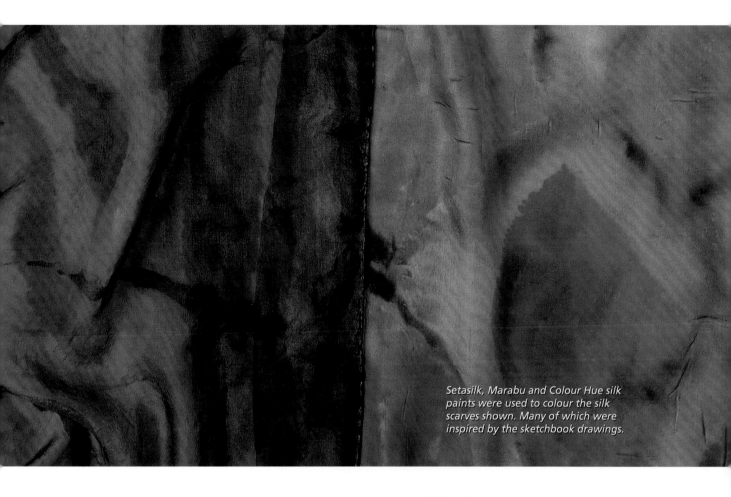

Setasilk, Marabu and Colour Hue silk paints were used to colour the silk scarves shown. Many of which were inspired by the sketchbook drawings.

To intensify the colour, a second application was applied. Incidentally, the coloured paper and newsprint used under the scarves to blot excess paint could be extremely useful for sketchbook or further design work.

Some of the fabric was deliberately folded, creased or rippled to allow the paint to drain in certain areas. Folding the material haphazardly while wet and before tumbling dry also produced unexpected organic markings.

All samples were iron fixed when dry. A gentle mild wash will restore the original softness of the silk.

Silk paint colour applied to a firmer silk could be quilted to decorate waistcoats, purses or cushions. A machined or hand stitched line would help to emphasise the fissures and indentations.

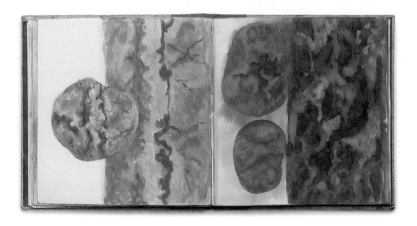

This page of small experimental 'notebook' samples includes; felt eroded with a heat tool and coloured with fabric paints, bonded with painted 'Tyvek', accented with dimensional paints and shapes cut out with a soldering iron. The grey and black samples illustrate the varying effects where grey 'Tyvek' has been bonded hard into different background fabrics: felt, a loose-weave cloth and a synthetic dupion. Layers of sheer or transfer painted synthetic fabric cut with a soldering iron are shown near bottom left of the page.

Erosion

Synthetic fabrics offer a wealth of opportunities for the creative embroiderer. They can be easily coloured with acrylic or fabric paints and transfer paints often transform them into unrecognisable and sumptuous cloths. (see book 4) One of their exciting attributes is that they react favourably when heat is applied as magical effects can be achieved.

Hot irons will shrink, blister, distress and melt certain synthetics. Varying the heat setting and the length of time, of ironing the fabric will also provide a variety of effects. Always remember to use baking parchment to protect the base of the iron.

Heat tools are much hotter than irons and dramatically distort, distress and erode synthetic materials. Different types of cloth will give a variety of results. Soldering irons used for stencil cutting can be extremely useful. Handled with care, intricate shapes and holes can be cut with the added advantage of sealing the edges of the cloth to reduce fraying.

Always follow safety precautions by wearing a mask or by working near an open door, window or preferably outside to prevent an adverse reaction from unexpected fumes or odours. When using heat or soldering irons, it is advisable for the fabric to be stretched tautly in a frame both to aid accuracy and for safety reasons.

Synthetic felt, such as 'Kunin', is now available from many craft suppliers. Originally designed for soft toy and doll making it has now become a useful addition to the embroiderers collection. Stretched tautly in a frame, a soldering iron with a clean, pointed tip can cut a fine network

of shapes. Alternatively, a heat tool can erode the surface effectively. It is wise to remember that these effects need to be incorporated into the intended piece and may need to be coloured. By dampening the surface, fabric or acrylic paints can be applied, burnished or smudged in to create an integrated finish. Felt may absorb the first application so this can be treated as a sealer and more applied to gain the desired effect.

Above: Inspired by the general characteristics of some of the stones illustrated right, this sample shows painted 'Tyvek' bonded onto felt that has been eroded with a heat tool. Dimensional glues were added to define some sections. Additional fabric paint was then applied to integrate the varying elements. Machine, hand stitches and beading were worked to accentuate or support the main area of interest.

Further metallic fabric paint was gently burnished to blend in selected areas. Lightly dampening the surface will help blend the colours. Incised lines made with a soldering iron suggested the cracks and fine fissures within the piece.

All three samples were inspired by the drawings shown above and were worked in pencil, aquarelle crayons and white gouache paint.

Below: *A synthetic dupion fabric was used as a ground fabric and the holes were cut with a soldering iron. The edges were bound and stitched with fine ribbons and wools incorporating small pieces of 'eroded' felt. The striped areas show strips of painted 'Tyvek' bonded hard to give a slightly distressed surface.*

Bottom Left: *This sample shows dark grey coloured 'Tyvek' bonded into the weave of the background material. A soldering iron was used to cut the main linear shapes from the 'Kunin' (synthetic felt) which were applied on top. Layers of eroded felt, machine stitching, running and seeding stitches were added to develop the image.*

'Tyvek' is another overused product that is seldom sympathetically placed within the work. However, if used with care it can have attractive qualities. It is often the case that the worker needs to be in control of the medium and not the other way round.

A subtle use of the softer material 'Tyvek' is to bond it on to the cloth. First paint one side with acrylic, permanent or metallic fabric paints, and leave to dry. Position a similar sized piece of 'Bondaweb' adhesive film taken from its paper backing and place under the 'Tyvek'

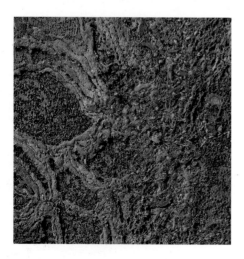

(painted side uppermost). Use backing parchment on top to protect the iron. With the iron set for cotton, iron very deliberately pressing very hard down on the material and firmly burnishing to break down and erode the surface into the backing fabric.

The temperature of irons varies so always be aware of this fact. A really hot iron will melt away the 'Tyvek' entirely! A cool iron used for adhering 'Tyvek' and Bondaweb to a ground cloth, generally results in softly indented surface that gives a smoother finish than the blistered or eroded surface created by a hot iron. 'Tyvek' and eroded felt can offer a very desirable partnership. After some practice, wonderfully understated, subtle organic, distressed surfaces can be achieved. Varying the type of fabric (See page 10) that you are applying the 'Tyvek' to, will also effect the result.

Given time to play and experiment, innovative surfaces can be created, especially when subtlety and discernment is applied. Always do this before embarking on an item whether it is a panel, bag, cushion or the like.

All samples and tryouts can be gathered in a notebook or on a notice board as an embroiderers 'thesaurus' for future use.

The techniques suggested could be partnered with hand or machine stitching but need to be part of the 'team' and not take over the starring role.

This Page: Grey coloured 'Tyvek' was bonded onto a background cloth and also to a piece of synthetic felt. This was then placed to create the dimensional layer. Using a warm iron only providing enough heat to adhere the fabrics one to another without distorting the 'Tyvek' too much. This action resulted in a slightly textured surface with a subtle sheen as suggested by the original observation of the stone.

Holes & Fissures

We can simulate the corrosive effect of the elements in many ways. 'Tyvek' can be very overused and obvious but it does have the amazing property of shrinking when heated. Used sensitively it can be incorporated in mixed media surfaces to good effect. This fossil piece (far right) is worked in lightweight 'Tyvek' and first painted and printed with various metallic surface paints. The machine stitching echoes the fossil sponge prints, being careful to link the shapes into an overall pattern. (fig 1 below)

Using a hot iron and a covering of baking parchment, the 'Tyvek' was ironed to melt into organic patterns with the machine stitch acting as a resist. (fig 2 far right)

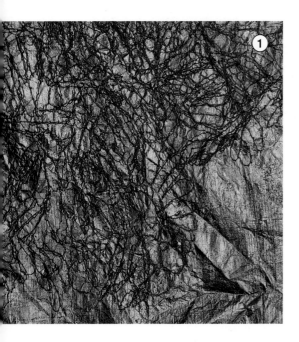

Right:
Painted 'Tyvek' was bonded on to felt to suggest an eroded effect and layered to form these intriguing surfaces. Machine stitching provided linear elements.

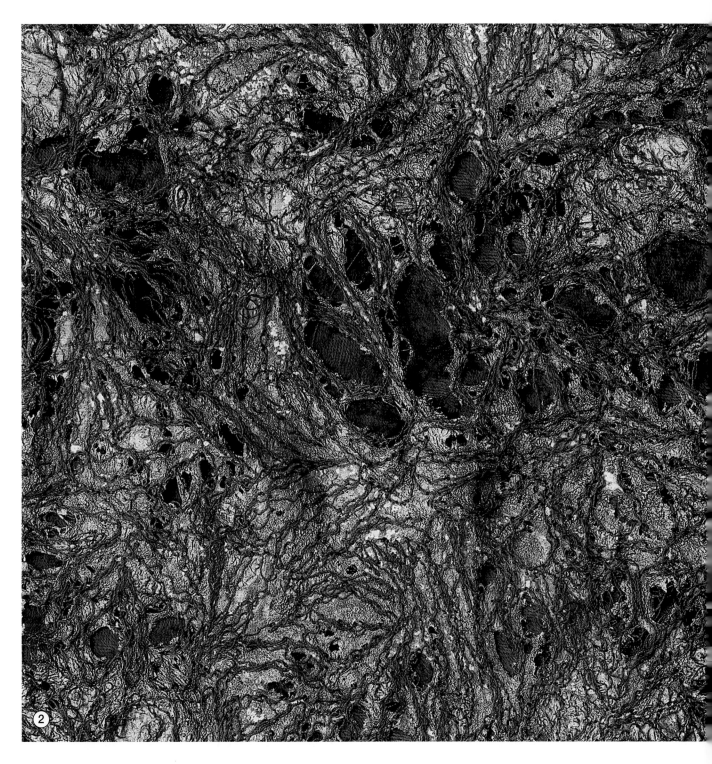

②

Synthetic materials respond to heat and we can use these properties to good effect.
The sample shown (fig 3 top left) comprises of four layers of synthetic velvet bonded together to give depth.
The surface has been ironed with a layer of 'Bondaweb' and then silver transfer foil ironed over using wool heat, no hotter. (see book 3)
Being aware of fumes and wearing a mask, a soldering tool was used to etch in the lines and textures. This is better worked with the fabrics stretched in a frame or on a metal tray.
It is possible to etch deep fissures and to rid the tool point of the sticky residue, switch off the power and clean using fine wire wool.
Surface paints or fine, transparent polyester scarves may be added to subdue the silver if desired.

Fossil Fabrics

Devoré paste was sponged carefully through the stencil to etch into the silk viscose velvet. (fig 1 below) After thorough cleaning it was also used to print discharge paste onto black cotton chiffon. (fig 2 below) In both cases the fabric has been left in it's original colour but could have been over dyed and printed.

When using the discharge paste note the way it varies when it dries out and the subtle effects that are possible. Some overprinting has taken place in order to achieve an 'in and out of focus' effect.
Fig 3 (right) displays a distressed pattern that has been worked on acrylic 'Kunin' felt. Silver transfer foil was first bonded onto the felt to achieve the silver metallic effect. Fabric paints were stencilled over the surface and machine stitching emphasised the shapes.
The machine stitching acted as a resist when the heat from a heat gun eroded the felt to give a distressed ancient fossil look. Patterns could also be made in a variety of ways including cut sponge foam blocks or string pattern blocks etc.

Always be aware when using chemicals to take full health and safety precautions.

It is still possible to walk along beaches such as Charmouth and find fossils that have been released from crumbling cliffs. These objects can hold a great fascination and provide the inspiration for patterns and surfaces.

They are infinitely variable in form, subtle colour and pattern and they could provide a lifetimes study. The dimensional elements can be a marvellous

resource for all kinds of surface stitching. They also lend themselves to repeating patterns because of their rhythmic simplicity.

The sketchbook illustrated (above) was the source of the fossil pattern that has been used for all the fabrics on this page. A simple stencil cut with a craft knife from stencil card is robust and can be used time and time again for a range of techniques.

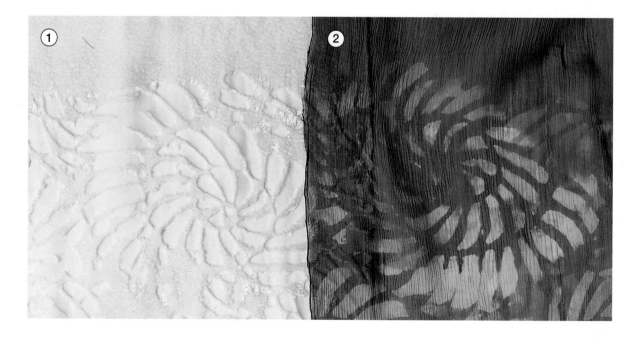

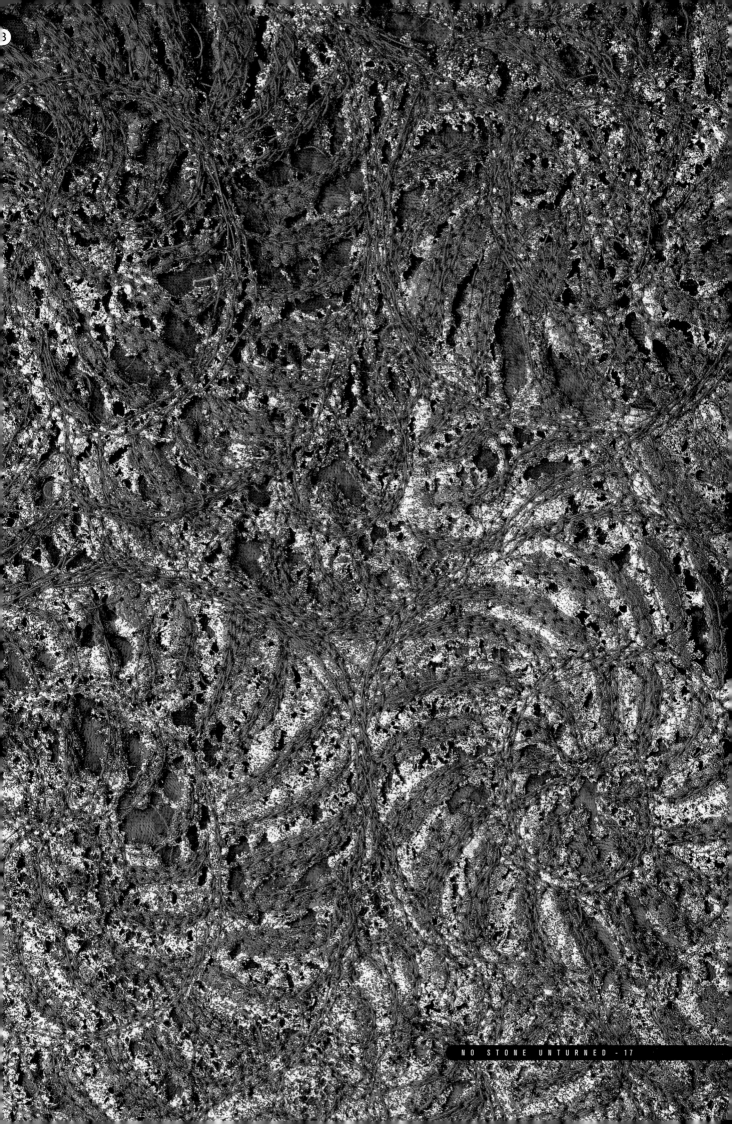

This staged sample shows the background fabric, first coloured with silk paint with some shapes depicted in a permanent silver paint. Areas of fabric have been haphazardly over sewn in a linen thread to depict the raised lines. Silver thread was then over stitched and knotted in places to develop the organic characteristics envisaged.

Ridges

Stones and pebbles display amazing networks of ridges and indentations. These can be interpreted in a number of ways.

By initially working in a fairly robust yarn, layers of line stitches can be worked one on top of another resulting in a strong structure with deep crevasses between. In order to emphasis the craggy, uneven surfaces, wrapping, knotting or beading into parts of the ridged stitching can accent these characteristics.

Pin tucks worked on a machine may will result in a pattern that appears too formal whereas tucks hand sewn can suggest a more organic and linear result.

Rouleaus (tubes of material) and some hollow knitting tapes can be filled with an appropriate sized thread and couched on to the surface.

Other options could be to couch garden twine, sisal, string, pipe cleaners, piping cord and the like to the ground fabric in the desired configuration. The whole surface can be covered with a softer fabric such as scrim, stitched and moulded over the lines to obtain a dimensional surface that can be a subtle, less obvious result. Italian quilting has a similar look but worked traditionally would not be so easy to interpret asymmetrical and uneven organic lines.

Dimensional paints and glues are now readily available in craft and hobby shops. Used with discretion, coloured and over stitched to integrate with the main design, these can be particularly successful when a finer tracery is required.

Ridges and layers created by machine stitching on soluble fabric offer a further choice. (see book 9)
Fine stitches, asymmetric shapes and non-fraying edges can be made using this method.

Machined cords, some of which may incorporate wire, offer another alternative. These too can be layered, adorned with beads, decorated with dimensional paints, wrapped, knotted or sewn down with some parts left raised from the fabric.

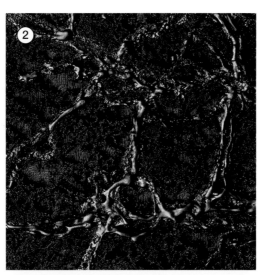

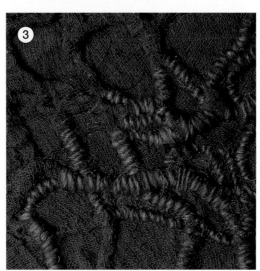

Fig 1: Layers of Romanian couching were worked on a soluble fabric. Knitting and weaving yarns were used to build a strong structure before selecting areas to be wrapped or beaded for highlights . Machine stitching was worked ensuing that all hand stitches were connected one to another before the 'background' was washed away.

Fig 2: Dimensional paints were applied in a fine tracery of lines on to heat-eroded felt. A first layer of fabric paints was applied to integrate the lines and the felt would have needed additional paint to blend more effectively if the sample had been worked further.

Fig 3: This partially worked sample illustrates how a thick string was couched on to a background fabric before being covered with scrims. These were stitched down along each side of the raised lines, some of which were then topped with straight stitches.

Below: The sketches of stones worked mainly in aquarelle crayons blended with water suggest patterns that could inspire.

Layers & Bumps

Holes in non synthetic fabrics can be cut, bound, machined or over sewn to prevent fraying. For certain effects, surrounding areas can be padded by quilting, trapunto or by layering small pieces of fabric and stitching them in place to achieve a dimensional surface.

Some hand stitching such as knotted buttonhole can be worked by layering the stitch in a haphazard way to form the high areas and machine stitching to 'quilt' or emphasise the lower cavities and fissures. To form a bumpy raised surface, layers of cross, sorbello or chain stitches can be worked in a bold knitting and weaving yarn to form a padding to be over stitched or wrapped for the final surface decoration.

Machine stitches onto soluble fabric to form a new cloth, is an extremely versatile technique. (see Books 1,9 & 10)

By first machining a mesh or network of stitches to ensure all areas are connected, layers of further stitching can be added on top to form a close or open fabric. During this process, snippets of thread or hand stitching can further develop the surface. The next stage is to dissolve the soluble fabric in water, stretch the new material to regain its shape and allow it to dry. Small pieces of this new material, which will not fray, can then be layered up to form the desired imagery. This approach affords the possibilities of making uneven, organic shapes that would be more difficult to achieve in other methods.

The lacy, holey qualities of this technique is also very attractive and designs inspired by the network of fissures to be found

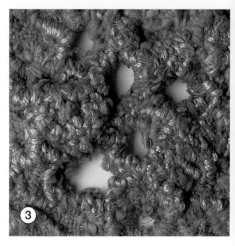

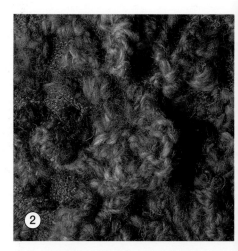

The three hand stitched samples illustrates exaggerated dimensional surfaces.

Fig 1: *Layers of cross and sorbello stitches were used as padding and decorated further with additional stitches, beads and wrappings. Worked in a soluble fabric and machined to connect all stitches.*

Fig 2: *Haphazard layers of knotted buttonhole with machine stitching 'quilting' the surfaces.*

Fig 3: *Layers of fabrics stitched to accentuate the bumps and bulges. A variety of matt and shiny threads were used to texture the top surface.*

Left: Machine stitches on soluble fabric created a new cloth for this little purse front that was inspired by the stone drawings. Separate pieces of newly created machined cloth, felt and hand stitches were worked to develop the surfaces. The non-fraying qualities of this technique facilitate intricate layering and the outside edges.

in many stones could certainly be adapted for decoration in fashion, clothes and accessories or within a panel.

Single lines of straight stitches connected to one another will result in a soft hanging, whereas lines which have been stitched several times or over stitched with a zigzag stitch will make a firmer structure. Adding hand stitching or beading before the dissolving process will give a stiffer finish that may well be suitable for certain items.

Very small snippets of fabric and thread, bonded to coloured and incised 'Tyvek' under a polyester 'chiffon' (see book 3) can give an attractive surface too. Remember to limit the snippets and not allow them to overlap the cuts in the 'Tyvek'. Iron very gently the top surface with just enough pressure to activate the 'Bondaweb', but not allowing

the 'Tyvek' to distort. At this stage carefully turnover the fabric and hover the iron over the fabric remembering to protect all surfaces with baking parchment. This action will encourage the 'Tyvek' to rise up towards the heat. Watch the action carefully through the parchment paper. Subtle,

undulating surfaces should show on the top-side. This method does take time to perfect but it can be a useful effect to incorporate into a piece of work.

Machine or hand stitching in the resulting crevasses will help emphasize these qualities.

Dimensional Stones

There is great pleasure to be had in picking up a stone to feel the surface. Touch is an important factor in the appreciation of its properties.

Making 3D stones can involve tactility and an awareness of the overall appearance of the object not as just a flat image.

The first stage is still to go back to the stone, look at the overall shape and note how the patterning is distributed over the entire surface.

A sketchbook devoted entirely to stones from a Samos beach has been a frequently used reference for a variety of textiles. (fig 1 top right)

Dry felting with a needle is excellent for creating dimensional organic forms. Careful placing and application of colour will make a beautiful soft textile stone that may be further enhanced by stitch. The core of these stones can be off cuts of wadding and unwanted wool fibres to make a base shape. Wool tops covering the surface become felted into the shape by constant pricking. (See dry felted necklace Page 2/3)

Bizarre as it may seem it is also possible to knit a stone. Take large needles and a chunky soft fibre and start knitting a loose square, about 20cms works well. Begin casting off and pick up chunks of the square before casting off more stitches and so on. The knitting will contort into an organic form. This will also make an excellent base for the dry felting process. (fig 2 left)

Stones can be used as a base for innovative moulding techniques. The glue used for these samples has been made with a tablespoon of PVA and a teaspoon of celulose paste to a pint of water. The celulose paste is available from art suppliers and does not contain anti-fungicidal so do not mix too much as it will not keep for more than a week.

When well mixed the materials will adhere together without them being so stiff that they lose their textile properties.

• First find a suitable stone and cover it in cling wrap. (fig 3 above)

• Glue the surface of the clingwrap and apply fabrics sensitively according to the striations and markings of the inspiration.

• Fine cottons, scrims and gauzes work particularly well, as synthetics can be difficult to stick. Papers and fibres may also be included.

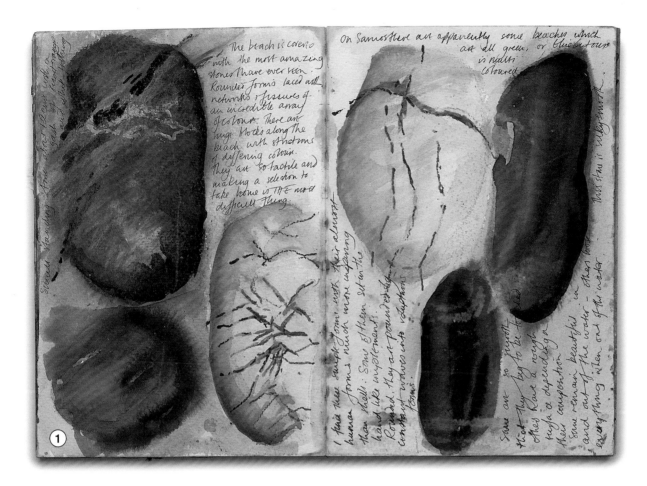

① *The beach is covered with the most amazing stones I have ever seen. Rounded forms laced with networks & fissures of an incredible array of colours. There are huge blocks along the beach with striations of differing colour. They are so tactile and making a selection to take home is THE most difficult thing.*

On Samos there are apparently some beaches which are all green, or blue & others is multi coloured

(handwritten marginal notes partially legible)

• The cotton scrims used for these stones have been dyed with hot water dyes, using several colours and transferring them from one pan to another to achieve more varied and subtle results.

• Apply two or three layers making sure to overlap the shapes.

• Moulding necessitates total involvement with the object and sensitivity to the contours and rhythms of the stone.

• Allow to dry and cut carefully.

• Cut enough to be able to remove the stone but it is not necessary to cut all the way round. (fig 3 top left)

• Stitching may be worked into the pliable surface. It could also be effective to work textures on soluble fabrics and then incorporate them into the surface. (see pages 20/21)

• The fabric stone may be padded and stitched or further gauzes glued to seal the join.

• The stitching of the join could become a feature of the surface.

Perhaps it could contain secrets and not be closed!
A collection of such fabric stones might make a simple but effective installation. (fig 4 below)

④

No Stone Unturned

The starting points offered in this book offer opportunities for embarking on what could be a lifetimes study.

We have both used images from our travels as well as inspiration from nearer to home.
When planning our books we hope to cover a range of methods from drawing and designing, colouring and preparing grounds through to machine and hand stitching. Music, poetry and prose can be the spur to inspire unusual ideas. Sometimes titles and phrases can spark a thought and not all work needs to have a serious content to be worthwhile.

Small scale items can have impact and on various courses where we have used stones and pebbles as a starting point, we have compiled lists of phrases, song titles etc that could be used to inspire a small piece of either 2D or 3D work.

They include:
• Blood from a stone
• Stone hearted
• Rock face
• Stone deaf
• Sticks & stones will break my bones
• Brimstone
• Gall stones

• A rolling stone gathers no moss
• Rock star
• Between a rock and a hard place
• Romancing the stone
• Vodka on the rocks
• Rock & Roll
• Stepping Stones

What is your response to these titles? Is there one that appeals to you?
Once you have started there is no end to this list.

Our fascination with rocks and stones will inevitably continue and we hope we have conveyed some of that enthusiasm to you along with some strategies for drawing, developing and working ideas on this fascinating subject.

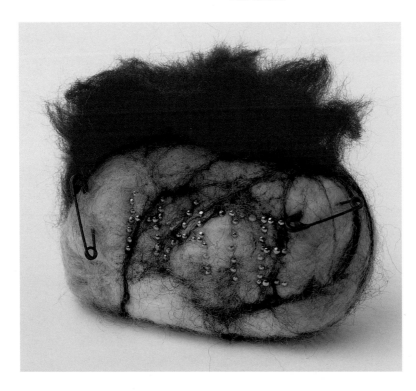

Top: Romancing the stone - Worked entirely in machine stitching on soluble fabric to form a new cloth. Inspired by a stone with a raised section partially worn away which was reminiscent of a heart shape. The edge displayed an interesting asymmetrical eroded pattern which inspired the decorative edging.

Left: Punk Rock - dry felted stone with pins and metal additions.